Accepting Yourself

Liking Yourself All of the Time

Dale R. Olen, Ph.D.

A Life Skills Series Book

JODA Communications, Ltd.
Milwaukee, Wisconsin

Editor: Carolyn Kott Washburne
Design: Chris Roerden and Associates
Layout: Eileen Olen

ISBN 1-56583-005-9

Published by: JODA Communications, Ltd.
10125 West North Avenue
Milwaukee, WI 53226

PRINTED IN THE UNITED STATES OF AMERICA

Table of Contents

Introduction

to the
Life Skills Series

Nobody gets out alive! It isn't easy navigating your way through life. Your relationships, parents, marriage, children, job, school, church, all make big demands on you. Sometimes you feel rather ill-equipped to make this journey. You feel as if you have been tossed out in the cold without even a warm jacket. Life's journey demands considerable skill. Navigating the sometimes smooth, other times treacherous journey calls for a wide variety of tools and talents. When the ride feels like a sailboat pushed by a gentle breeze, slicing through the still waters, you go with the flow. You live naturally with the skills already developed.

But other times (and these other times can make you forget the smooth sailing), the sea turns. The boat shifts violently, driven by the waves' force. At those stormy moments, you look at your personal resources, and they just don't seem sufficient.

Gabriel Marcel, the French philosopher, wrote that the journey of life is like a spiral. The Greeks, he observed, viewed life as *cyclical*–sort of the same old thing over and over. The seasons came, went, and came again. History repeated itself. The Hebrews, on the other hand, saw life as *linear*–a pretty straight march toward a goal. You begin at the Alpha point and end at Omega. It's as simple as that.

Marcel combined the two views by capturing the goal-oriented optimism of the Hebrews and the sobering reality of the Greeks' cycles. Life has its ups and downs, but it always moves forward.

To minimize the *downs* and to make the most of the *ups*, you need **Life Skills**. When you hike down the Grand Canyon, you use particular muscles in your back and legs. And when you trudge up the Canyon, you use other muscles. So too with life skills. You call on certain skills when your life spirals down, such as the skill of defeating depression and managing stress. When your life is on an upswing, you employ skills like thinking reasonably and meeting life head on.

This series of books is about the skills you need for getting through life. To get from beginning to end without falling flat on your face and to achieve some dignity and some self-satisfaction, you need **basic** life skills. These include:

1. Accepting yourself.
2. Thinking reasonably.
3. Meeting life head on.

With these three life skills mastered to some degree, you can get a handle on your life. Now, if you want to build from there, you are going to need a few more skills. These include:

4. Communicating.
5. Managing stress.
6. Being intimate.
7. Resolving conflict.
8. Reducing anger.
9. Overcoming fear.
10. Defeating depression.

If you have these ten skills up and running in your life, you are ready to face yourself, your relationships, your parents, your marriage, your children, your job and even God with the hope of handling whatever comes your way. Without these skills, you are going to bump into one stone wall after another. These skills don't take away the problems, the challenges and the hard times. But they do help you dig out of life's deep trenches and more fully *enjoy* the good times.

Life Skills can be learned. You have what it takes to master each of these skills—even if you feel you don't have the tiniest bit of the skill right now. But nobody can develop the skill for you. You have to take charge and develop it yourself. Your family, friends and community may be able to help you, but you are the center at which each skill has to start. Here is all you need to begin this learning process:

- Awareness.
- The desire to grow.
- Effort and practice.

Awareness begins the process of change. You have to notice yourself, watch your behavior and honestly face your strengths and weaknesses. You have to take stock of each skill and of the obstacles in you that might inhibit its growth.

Once you recognize the value of a skill and focus on it, you have to want to pursue it. The critical principle here, one you will see throughout this series, is *desire*. Your desire will force you to focus on the growing you want to do and keep you going when learning comes hard.

Finally, your *effort and practice* will make these **Life Skills** come alive for you. You can do it. These books are tools to guide and encourage your progress. They are my way of being with you— cheering your efforts. But without your practice, what you find in these books will wash out to sea.

Working on these ten **Life Skills** won't get you through life without any scars. But the effort you put in here will help you measure your life in more than years. Your life will be measured in the zest, faith, love, honesty and generosity you bring to yourself and your relationships.

I can hardly wait for you to get started!

Chapter One

The Skill of Accepting Yourself

f you master this skill, you will master them all. Sure, you still have to work at the others, but accepting yourself makes that work much easier. This business of liking yourself touches all of us at some point in our lives. For some people negative self-esteem pursues relentlessly and constantly; for others, only occasionally. But it lurks there for all of us, ready to undercut our sense of worth and value.

The skill of accepting yourself is simple to explain but more difficult to develop than many other life skills. You know you have it if you like yourself. You wouldn't trade yourself in for a different model. Oh sure, you might want to barter some parts for qualities or talents you see in others, but overall you like who you are and are comfortable being you.

When you're self-accepting you feel *secure*. You act confidently and assertively, because you realize no one can take from you your sense of self. You believe that no one can reach in and pull from you the deepest parts of your self. You're not dependent on others for your acceptance. Certainly you want others to like you and approve of your work, but if they don't, you still stand tall. You don't get blown away by the disapproval of another. Your esteem stands on its own strength and is impenetrable to the reactions of others. That's self-acceptance which leads to self-love, which leads to positive self-esteem.

That last sentence contained all the terms generally used in connection with this issue. Often, counselors and writers make distinctions among these terms, showing you the differences and similarities. I don't think that's very important for developing the skill of accepting yourself. These terms all work together. Basically the skill involves accepting your pluses and minuses, liking who you are overall and thinking well of yourself. Call all that what you will. Here I'm calling it the *skill of accepting yourself.*

Self-acceptance is born of the messages you receive from your parents.

From childhood Lisa heard the message, "You will be liked if you are cute." Her mother always dressed her in the prettiest clothes, curled her hair perfectly every day, put make-up on her when she was four, had her ears pierced at five and by six was telling her to watch her diet. When Lisa got messy playing with friends, she received subtle, disapproving messages, implying that young ladies don't do such things and that they always look nice.

When Lisa grew up, she had a little trouble with weight. She struggled with an extra 15 pounds that, she thought, made her look terrible. At those times she brought up her childhood belief – "You are liked if you are cute" – and she came to the logical conclusion:

"If I'm overweight then I'm not cute. If I'm not cute, then others don't like me. If I'm not liked, then I'm not good. I don't accept myself this way; I don't like myself this way. I'm not a lovable person this way."

Lisa perceived certain *facts:* she had gained 15 pounds. She no longer fit into her size 8 pants. She was, in fact, eating more between meals. These facts remained neutral. They were neither right nor wrong in themselves.

But next Lisa began *self-talk*. She discussed these facts within herself, beginning to lay interpretations over the facts to make sense out of them. She said, "I wonder if others will think I'm ugly now. I have these huge bulges. I must look just awful. Everyone else looks so much better than I do. I don't have any control over myself any more. What if I keep getting fatter and fatter?"

Lisa's self-talk set up the next step, namely *judgments*. She quickly came to conclusions based on the facts and her interpretative self-talk. She concluded:

- I am ugly.
- I am not likable while fat.
- I am a piece of junk.

After Lisa had 1) perceived the facts, 2) talked to herself about those facts and 3) passed judgment on those facts and interpretations, she *reacted*. She felt depressed. She quit trying to diet and went on an eating binge. This depressed her more. Soon she got into the pattern of depression, binge eating and more depression. Each time the cycle occurred, she beat up on herself a little more. She didn't accept herself. In fact, she hated herself this way.

She developed low self-esteem, because early in life she received significant messages that tied self-acceptance to her physical appearance. Just as easily she could have received a hundred other messages battering her self-esteem, such as:

- If people don't pay attention to me, then I don't count.
- If I make a mistake, I am a failure.
- I'm a good person if I please my parents (or others).
- I'm good when I'm successful.
- If I don't accomplish certain things, I'm terrible.
- If others get upset with me, it's my fault and I'm bad.

The more positive and unconditional the messages you received in childhood, the more you accept yourself. The key to positive self-esteem lies in being loved by parents without conditions. You are good just because you exist – and not because you got straight A's, did the dishes without complaining or won the student-body elections. If you were loved without having to *prove* you were a worthwhile creature, then you have one leg up on the skill of self-acceptance.

Self-acceptance means embracing *all* of yourself.

Acceptance goes well beyond tolerance. It involves the gracious embracing of the self. You can "accept" (bear with) a cold or the flu. You can grit your teeth when the neighbor is bragging *again* about his daughter's grades in school. You can "grin and bear it" when your perfectionistic boss criticizes your work because some picky little detail is out of place. You tolerate these situations. You live with them.

However, when it comes to yourself, you need more than mere tolerance. It's not sufficient to "live with" yourself in a begrudging manner. Self-acceptance calls for a loving action, whereby you take yourself to your heart and say "yes." It means affirming whatever you find there. You don't need to love or "be thrilled" with everything you discover about yourself. But you do need to see it all as one package–a package that you lovingly embrace with all its beauty and ugliness.

Self-acceptance especially means embracing the dark side of yourself.

When two people get married they are asked to accept each other in good times and bad. Can they accept one another's limitations as well as strengths? If they can, then this couple has a great chance at a successful relationship. Why? Because they have completed the "project of ambivalence." This project is a task that every adult must accomplish to live a satisfying and fulfilling life. At some point in your life you run smack into your own limitedness. You are faced with the same issue as the married couple. Can you love, cherish and embrace yourself with your limits and your strengths? Can you enter your dark side, face what's there and continue to lovingly accept who you are?

Jill was a giving person. Not only did she advocate for social programs to help the poor, but she herself worked regularly at a meal program and in a community advocacy center. She committed her time, money and energy to these generous works. She felt good about what she was doing. Then one day she experienced a gnawing feeling – she wanted something back. She began to realize that she herself wanted gratitude and recognition for all she was doing. She started resenting people who didn't notice how much she was doing for them. She wanted appreciation for all the good work she had done.

Those new feelings scared her. She never felt that way before. She began feeling guilty, which is a sure sign of non-acceptance. She didn't like feeling guilty. She didn't think much of herself for feeling the need for recognition. She fought against those feelings and thoughts. They persisted. She felt worse and worse, thinking she was some kind of selfish person. She couldn't accept herself as a person whose generosity might have a self-serving aspect.

Only when Jill began to see how normal such feelings were and that those feelings did not make her a bad person could she begin the process of self-acceptance. Eventually, by facing her dark feelings, she began to embrace them. She still wished they weren't there, but she understood her own human limitedness and need. She recognized that these dark places in her were simply part of what made her who she was.

To fully accept yourself, you need to enter into and face your own dark side, at some point in your life. Speaking of this shadowy aspect in the abstract may make it sound mysterious and eery. What ominous creatures lurk deep within your heart? You may not want to face what lies in the deep crevices of your soul.

People who take the journey into their shadow often find it difficult. But they also discover a rich dimension to their lives that yields a fuller appreciation and love of themselves. I once worked with a man, Mike, who came face to face with his darkness. He discovered a violence within that actually made him tremble. He couldn't believe it. He had always thought of himself as a peaceful man. He could not fit his attraction toward violence with his peaceful beliefs and behaviors. He wondered who the stranger within him was.

He realized how he talked against violence on television and in the movies. Yet when no one was around, he'd watch it himself. He read about violent crimes in the papers and magazines. He found himself fascinated from a distance. He further recognized the depth of his own inner rage. Sure, he had it under control, but it was there and powerful. It went way back to his teen years, when he felt actual hatred for a teacher and a couple of bully students.

When Mike entered this darkness, he wanted to deny it, fight against its presence. But he stayed with it. He entered it without acting upon it. He began to accept it as simply a part of himself. He could control it, but it was there. Gradually he began embracing it, not out of joy, but with respect and even reverence. Finally he passed through the darkness and came again into the light of his life. He then knew both sides of himself, the light and the dark.

Later he described the experience as one that added tremendous depth to his life. He said:

"Accepting the dark side was like painting. If I paint only with primary colors, I can make nice pictures. That's like accepting just the bright side of myself. But if I take the darker colors – the browns, blacks and grays – and mix them with the primaries, I add a much richer tone to my painting. I add depth, strength and power. I don't particularly like that dark side of myself when it stands alone, but I accept it as an important part of who I am."

Self-acceptance, then, means saying "yes" to all that makes you who you are. Understanding and acceptance leads you to appreciate yourself, to judge yourself positively and to celebrate who you are and the world in which you live. Now, let's turn to the *how* of self-acceptance. The journey takes work and effort, but the results make the trip worthwhile.

Chapter Two

Principles and Tools for Accepting Yourself

Principle 1

**Self-acceptance and self-esteem are found
within yourself, not outside of yourself.**

I met a man years ago. He claimed to be a gold prospector.

I asked: "How long have you been searching for gold?"

He told me with pride rising in his voice: "Goin' on 40 years."

I pressed the dialogue: "How successful have you been?"

"Well, I'm still looking. I haven't found any gold yet," he said.

"Really," I responded, astonished at his perseverance: "Where do
you look for gold?"

"On the streets of the city," he said in all seriousness.

All I could say was "Oh."

I walked away stunned that a man could spend his life looking for a treasure in the wrong field. I wanted to take him by the shoulders, shake him and yell, "You're looking in the wrong place. Gold is not buried in city streets. Gold is in fields, often near rivers and streams, often buried deep within the earth's center. If you're going to spend your life looking for a treasure, at least look where you have a chance of finding it."

Self-esteem is the treasure many people look for in the wrong field. They seek it in the approval of others and in their own external successes. The task of this book is to help you discover self-worth *within* yourself rather than from out there some place. It can be hard to shift your focus from outside to inside, but that's the work that lies before you.

One of the most important tasks of your childhood was adapting to and fitting into the world around you. You had to learn the rules of how to act in the world. You had to become sensitive to the ways people talked to one another, the ways they acted toward each other and the ways they tried to gain the positive responses of other people. In a word, you made great efforts to figure out how the world operated and how you could achieve happiness in it.

You focused, then, on what happened around you. You paid close attention to how other people reacted to you when you smiled, frowned, cried, spit, expressed affection, stood on your head, talked in class and slurped your soup. Sometimes people responded positively, other times negatively, and still other times with a yawn and a turned back. Some people never even noticed.

When they reacted positively, you liked it. You felt good about yourself. You began thinking, "Gee, I must be a pretty good guy if they like me and praise me." When people reacted negatively, you easily began thinking, "Gee, maybe I'm not such a nice guy. Look how they acted toward me." Your self-esteem got connected to other people's reactions to you.

Then you learned an important, although faulty, lesson: "People think well of me when I perform well. Therefore, I must perform well to be liked by others. And if others like me, then I can like myself." No. Please unlearn that terrible belief. Self-esteem cannot be found in the field of other people's acceptance. The treasure of self-worth lies within your own heart.

Certainly, other people's affirmation and love serve as critical pieces for your self-esteem. Without such positive responses early in life, you fight an uphill battle in your struggle for self-esteem. You need to be given the gift of self-love by the unconditional love of your parents. But once that love has been experienced, you cannot continue to rely on the love and approval of others for your sense of self-worth. You cannot depend on other people's reactions to you in order to feel good about yourself.

At some point your attention needs to be re-directed to yourself and to what operates deep within you. In fact, this re-focusing stands as the central midlife task. The crisis of midlife directs you from an outer focus to an inner focus. I see this task as the major conversion point in your life. No other work is as significant to your living a full human life.

Principle 2

All creation is made up of outer and inner voices. Learn to listen most attentively to your own inner voice.

Western people often think of creation as made up of matter – good, hard material stuff you can get your hands on. What exists you can grab onto; you can touch it and smell it and bump against it.

Eastern people, on the other hand, often think of creation as made up of *sound*. The world is a voice, the vibrations of which fill the universe with life.

For a while I'd like to invite you to think a bit like an Easterner might think. Listen to the world as made up of voices. You have heard these voices since infancy. They came from your parents and siblings and relatives. They inundated you from the television and radio and movie theater. They filled your head in the school room, on the ball field and in the church sanctuary.

All these voices shaped and formed your thinking and your behavior. You took them in, believing many of them, rejecting many others. Your ears have become sensitively tuned to hear those voices, much like a mother hears the cry of her own child amid the din of playground noise. The outer voices speak, you listen up. They play a hypnotic tune that finds its way deep within you. They shout their message, demanding you pay attention and consent.

While these outer voices speak and seduce, there whispers a quiet voice from the deepest recesses of your being. This voice proclaims a powerful message but one that cannot be easily heard against the noise and din of the outer world voices. It is easily drowned out by the cacophony of sound from outside. The work of self-acceptance is to learn how to hear and listen to this inner voice, this whisper that arises from your heart.

Such an effort makes you "counter-cultural." Our society allows itself to be directed from the outside. It listens to and tends to believe the powerful voices of the rich and famous. It attends to the messages of news anchors and commercial endorsements by sports figures. It takes in what authoritative church officials say and what politicians promise.

Your efforts in reaching for higher levels of self-acceptance and esteem will allow you to turn away from these voices as the primary authority in your life. Your efforts will, instead, direct you toward your own heart. You will grow quiet within, gradually turning down the volume of the outer world, and listen – listen well – to the voice that whispers from your heart.

I don't want to give you the impression that all outer voices give negative, awful messages. On the contrary, many outer voices speak the same message as that of your heart. But to know which voices resonate in harmony and which do not, you first need to know and attend to that inner voice. Once you have listened well to your inner voice, you will be able to sort the outer voices that magnify the voice within from those that cause dissonance with your heart's whisper.

Principle 3

Your inner voice can be framed also as the voice of God or of your Higher Power.

Religious people of all ages have believed in a creator God. Such a belief can help you gain a better sense of your inner voice. If God has created, then you must contain an element of God. The artist leaves a part of him or herself in every painting.

In many religious traditions God is viewed as a *loving*, creative power. Such a view allows you to realize that at the core of your being you are the result of love. The action of love begets goodness. At your center, then, you are fundamentally good because you have been loved into existence by a loving creator. The voice that speaks at the core of you can be heard also as the voice of God.

Quite honestly, starting with this type of belief makes it somewhat easier to journey inward. If you begin the journey believing that you will find goodness, you will be more motivated to travel to your heart. The voice that speaks there announces your worth and value. It speaks positively and with energy about your goodness and power.

Principle 4

Your inner voice speaks of positive energies.

I would like you to believe that the journey to your heart ends in a wonderful discovery of your goodness. Now if you have spent much of your life believing you aren't worth anything, then you won't easily trust that goodness can be found inside. I want you to doubt that thought, because your negative beliefs about self certainly haven't helped you much anyway. In fact, they have been the source of considerable pain to you. So why not start out trying to believe – taking it on faith – that maybe you will find a treasure at your heart.

Over the years I have recognized three views that people take toward what lies at their heart. Some people believe that bad stuff sloshes around down there. They imagine fiery balls or black tar pits or rotten globs of slime. They are convinced that to journey there will only make them feel worse. What they think is at their heart scares them off. They don't want anything to do with those dark and dank recesses of their being.

A second group of people believes that *nothing* will be found if they enter their heart. They feel devoid of good or bad. They experience themselves as hollow, empty people. They fear going to their heart because it will only confirm their shallow experience of life. In some ways this position may be the most frightening. These people sense their emptiness, but don't have to face it if they never look inward.

Finally, there are those who believe that goodness reigns at their heart. They have experienced some level of self-affirmation. They have had some taste of "the good life." They know it's there. They liked it and want to pursue it. They have some confidence that the journey will pay rich dividends.

It's this last position that I want you to take as you begin this journey. If you cannot get yourself to that place, then I invite you to take the chance that I am right – that there is an inner richness at your heart that you have already experienced over and over but have not attended to.

The belief I would like you to start with is this:

> At your heart lie fundamentally good energies, created in you from the beginning. These are not powers that you earned. They came with your existence. They are built in. These energies or movements continually urge you toward freedom and love. They call you to live fully, to live in peace, contentment and joy. These energies cannot be taken from you in any way. You are the energies of your heart. Since they are fundamentally good, so are you.

Principle 5

**Your outer voices are made up of all the messages you
have received throughout your life and
incorporated within.**

Think of the ways you learn things over the years. Your senses act like a vacuum cleaner, taking in whatever is offered. As time goes on you become more discriminating about what messages you accept and what you reject. Many messages, however, sneak in without you even being aware of them. Advertising uses the sneaky approach by sending so many messages that some just stick. If you throw enough mud, some remains on the wall.

So the messages come in from all sides. They come directly from the words others have spoken to you. They come from television, radio, music, books. And they come from your experiences. All these messages enter your inner world. They find a home and begin influencing the movement of your heart's energies.

Many of these outer voices speak in harmony with your inner voice. But many do not speak the same language or send the same message. Some of the messages you learned that resonate well with your inner voice include the following:

- I am lovable as I am.
- Other people enjoy being with me.
- No matter what I do, Dad and Mom love me.
- I want to make and follow my own decisions.
- I enjoy helping other people when they are in need.

These voices match your heart and magnify your heart's voice. They tell you of your own basic goodness and your basic orientation toward life rather than death.

There are other voices, however, that cause dissonance. These voices sound strident when set against the voice within. Some of these messages include:

- What other people think of me is most important.
- I must always make a good impression on others.
- Strong feelings are wrong and should be repressed.
- I must always act in perfect ways.
- It is critical to succeed in order to like myself.
- If I speak up, people will think I am dumb.
- Others are always better than me.

Many of these positive and negative voices have been speaking to you for years. They have become so much a part of your background noise that you no longer even pay attention to them. They register in you like elevator music – it's always there, but you don't notice it. In psychology we refer to these background sounds as "automatic beliefs." They automatically arise in you when the right circumstance comes up. The neighbor gets a new expensive car. You feel a little depressed. An automatic belief surfaces: "Others always do better than me." That little message, then, affects your mood as well as your feelings about yourself.

Basically you need to identify your positive beliefs and messages, reinforce them and eliminate those negative beliefs that pounce whenever they get a chance. By getting rid of those negative beliefs, you give the whispers of your heart – those positive, wonderful energies – a chance to be heard. They can speak to you of who you are, and they can call you to act in ways that enliven you and others.

Principle 6

You need to know the relationship between the outer voices and the energies of the heart.

So now you know you have outside voices and inside voices. "So what?" you might be thinking. I want to show you so what. I want you to know how these two aspects of your life interact and determine your identity, your behaviors, and your feelings.

You begin your life with the energies of your heart. Deep within you lie these movements that are fundamentally good and powerful. As you age, these energies grow. You are born with these energies. They come with the territory of human nature.

As soon as you enter the world, these energies begin to be layered over by the outer voices. These voices become your beliefs. They enter you. Many of them settle in your unconscious mind, where they have an impact on your behaviors and feelings, often without your awareness.

Picture yourself as a cone.

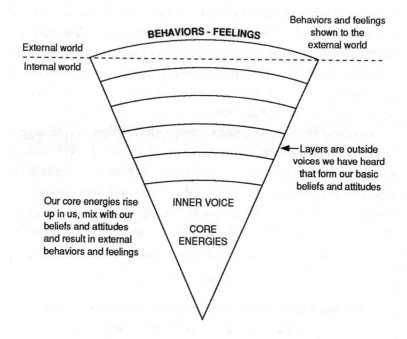

(Similar graphs first appeared in my book *Whispers of the Heart,* Resource Publications, Inc., 1987.)

At the bottom of this cone lies the core of your rich energies. The outer voices, your learned beliefs, cover those core energies. At the top of the cone you find your behaviors and your feelings. These are what others see of you and you of them. All the layers and the core energies are hidden from the view of the world. What shows of the real you, the full you, consists in your behavior and your feelings. Yes, you are much like the iceberg that only shows the top layer of a much larger reality.

Now, your behaviors and feelings are created from the mix of your heart's energies and the layers of belief that cover them. Remember, some of those layers are facilitating and harmonious layers. They assist the energies of your heart to rise up, come to the surface, and show themselves through healthy behaviors and feelings. Other layers or beliefs, however, retard and sabotage those deep energies. They deflect the energies on their way to the surface, causing them to appear in contradictory and confusing ways. Your behavior and feelings then appear not to match the energies that flow from your heart.

If your layers or beliefs are in harmony with your heart, then the flow of energy is direct and true. The layers help the energies come to the surface.

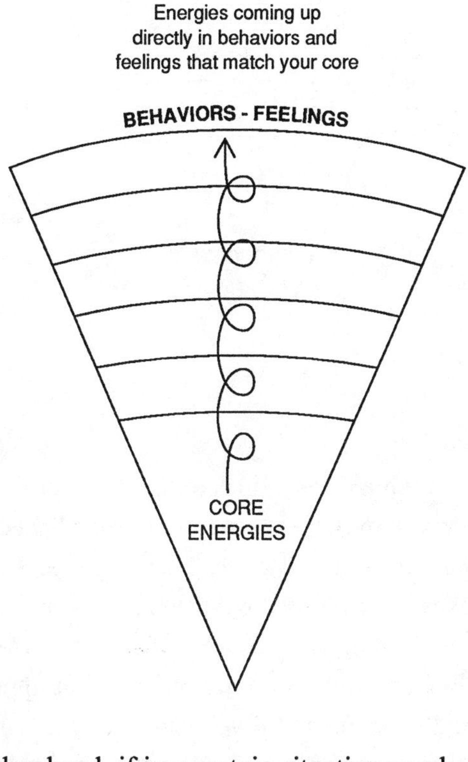

Energies coming up
directly in behaviors and
feelings that match your core

BEHAVIORS - FEELINGS

CORE
ENERGIES

On the other hand, if in a certain situation you have layers that don't match your heart, those layers will constrain and detour your good energies on their way to the surface. In the diagram below you see the energy being thrown off course by restrictive and sabotaging layers. The behaviors and the feelings you have don't match, in these cases, with the movements of your heart.

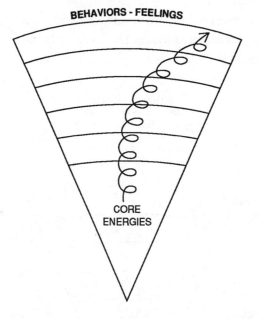

Let's take a couple of examples to see this more clearly.

Deep within you moves the energy of love. Placed in you from the moment you came into existence, this energy seeks to come to the surface and express itself in loving behaviors and feelings. For example, you're walking along a downtown street when you notice a woman who looks worried and quite agitated. You approach her and ask if something is wrong and if you can be of assistance. She tells you she is visiting your city and her eight-year-old son has just disappeared. You ask his name, she tells you and the two of you begin calling out, "Jason, Jason!" Shortly Jason strolls out of a little electronics shop and returns to his mother's side. All ends happily.

Your behaviors – approaching the woman, asking if she needed help, taking the time to help her – are all loving behaviors. They flowed directly from that deep, loving energy created in you at the moment of your conception. Most, if not all, of the layers or beliefs you had about helping people in need aided your loving energy in coming up directly and positively. Some of those facilitating beliefs might have been:

- You should always help those in need.
- Helping another is more important than getting to a meeting on time.
- It is safe to approach a strange woman but not a strange man.
- People in need welcome others help.
- You should love your neighbor as yourself.

These kinds of beliefs obviously assist your loving energy in coming directly to the surface and showing itself in caring behavior. You have attained a very nice match between the energy of your heart and what shows to the world, namely, your behavior. You are in harmony with yourself.

Take the same scenario, only this time imagine that you have a different set of beliefs (layers) covering that loving energy in your heart. Imagine you learned to believe the following:

- You should be very careful about whom you help.
- The meeting I'm going to is more important than this person's problem.
- It's potentially dangerous dealing with any stranger, man or woman.
- Most people don't want strangers butting into their business.
- It's best to stay out of other people's affairs.

Given this set of beliefs, what would happen to the loving energy of your heart? It would come up in an indirect and confusing way.

You would see the woman on the street looking worried and agitated. You would walk right past her to your meeting. However, as you passed by, and for much of the day, you would feel little pangs of guilt because you didn't stop to help. So at the top of your cone shows the behavior of walking by and the feeling of guilt. At the bottom of you moves the energy of love and care. These don't match each other very well. Your beliefs detoured your loving energy, so what came out was avoidant behavior and guilty feelings.

You can see from this example that your behaviors and feelings, then, are created by the mix of your basic, good core energies and the beliefs you have accumulated throughout your life. Your beliefs and feelings are what shows to world. This is what others see of you. Based on what they see, they determine *who* you are. But notice that your behaviors and feelings make up a very tiny aspect of the whole you. You are so much more than your behaviors and feelings.

You can now identify three aspects of yourself. There are your *core energies* which are very good. There are your *beliefs,* many of which resonate in harmony with your core energies and many of which sound dissonant with the whisper of your heart. And there are your *behaviors* and *feelings* – the surface you. This is the most visible part, and so, the part you and all the rest of us focus on the most.

Principle 7

**Feelings are not part of your core energy. They exist at
the outer edge of your being.**

"Your feelings lie deep within you" is a belief held by most of us. In fact, you probably learned that if you get "in touch" with your feelings, you really come to know yourself. Wrong! Contrary to popular belief, your feelings stand as an external expression of yourself. They live at the top of you (at the top of the cone), not at the core. During the 1960s and the 1970s, feelings were "in." We all thought that by getting in touch with feelings, we would come to know ourselves deeply. I think we have now found out this is not necessarily true.

In the past we said, "If you know your feelings, you know yourself." It's more accurate to say, "If you know your feelings, then you know your feelings." It's very important for you *not* to equate your feelings with your identity. You are not your feelings. You are not your behavior, either. You are not your beliefs or layers. No. Instead, *you are the energies of your heart.*

Your feelings certainly are important. They serve as *signals,* either direct or indirect, of the movements of your heart. Your warm affection, for example, serves as a direct signal of your loving energy. Your anger or guilt can act as an indirect signal of that same loving energy. But you are not your warm affection nor are you your anger or guilt. You are so much more than that. Those emotions ebb and flow. They change. Your identity is not so volatile. It is constant. And what is constant in you is your basic, good energies. You are your energies, then. You are *not* your emotions.

Principle 8

Self-acceptance and self-esteem are based on your ability to focus on your core energies rather than on your behaviors or feelings.

You get a message at work that the boss wants to see you at 3:30 today. You know there have been rumors of layoffs. But you also know you have been doing a very good job. You're not sure what the meeting is all about. As the day goes on, you focus more and more on the possibility of getting laid off. You're pretty new on the job. You don't have much seniority. You're not really part of the "in" crowd. You spend the day worrying about the meeting, already planning what you will say when told you have been laid off. You have even been figuring out what companies you will apply to next.

The hour arrives. With considerable anxiety and trepidation you knock on the ominous door. The guillotine could not have been worse. The boss welcomes you warmly, invites you to sit down and compliments you on the work you have been doing. The sure "kiss of death." You clench your teeth, ready for the blade to drop. The word "but" always follows such compliments. You feel sick and weak.

However, the "but" never comes. The boss tells you about an opportunity with the company in Germany for two years. He thinks you're the person for the job. Would you consider it? You're stunned. You have to readjust your entire focus. By 3:30 you had gotten yourself worked up to the point of quitting before you got laid off. Now the boss is asking if you'd like an advancement in the company and a great experience in Germany for two years.

You spent your entire day worrying yourself into high blood pressure. By the time of the meeting you had eliminated any chance that something positive would result. What happened to you during the day brings me to one of the educational crescendos of this book. Here it is: *You give power to what you focus on.*

You could have focused on the good work you had been doing and anticipated a positive meeting with the boss. If you had, your day would have been much more peaceful. But you focused, instead, on what might go wrong. That caused unnecessary worry. You wasted much psychic energy.

Whatever you focus on, attend to, concentrate on, you give that part of reality power in your life. Now apply this most important principle to self-acceptance. In forming your identity and accepting who you are, you can focus on your *behaviors* and your *emotions,* or you can focus on the *energies* of your heart. It's your choice. I can assure you, however, that the more you attend to the energies of your heart, the more power you give those energies. And the more power you experience at the core of you, the more likely you learn to celebrate your goodness. You sense your goodness as a person because you know the energies of your heart in a strong and rich way.

The task, then, is to focus on your inner energies and to *disconnect* from any outer focus. As you journey inward, you place less importance on your behaviors and other people's reactions to you. These become secondary in helping you accept yourself as a worthwhile person. You *are* worthwhile because you possess powerful, good energies that are always moving within you. These energies do not depend on your successes or failures nor on the adulation or criticism of others. They simply exist as part of you, permanently and powerfully.

Principle 9

To enter your heart, begin with your behaviors and feelings.

Sure, I want you to focus on your core energies. I want you to learn to uncouple yourself from too much attention to your behaviors and feelings. But to get started on the journey inward, you need to begin where you live, which is in your behaviors and feelings. These serve as signals that carry you to your inner life. As signals, *all* your behaviors and feelings are good. They point you, either directly or indirectly, to their source – the powers of your heart.

Remember, your behaviors and feelings operate at the top of you. These are the parts of you that show to the world. They are the easiest for you to identify and corral. Once you recognize these signals, you begin the journey to your heart. You will enter into and pass through the many layers of belief that stand between you and your core energies. As you move through these belief layers, you will finally come to pay dirt. You will touch the deepest energies of your being. Once you get there, you will then be able to celebrate the real you. For you are the energies of your heart.

Chapter Three

A Structured Approach to the Heart

Principle 10

There are two ways to reach the heart. First, you can proceed, layer by layer, in a cognitive, structured way. Second, you can move in a less structured, more intuitive way.

In this chapter I'll show you the more cognitive approach, and in Chapter Four I'll show you the more intuitive approach.

Let's get right to the structured process. It's Sunday evening. The sun died several hours ago. The house feels damp and cold. The kids are fighting in some distant room. Tom sinks deeper in his chair. He senses his life energy slowly draining from his body. He stares at the television without really seeing it. Gloom settles over him like grimy oil on the beaches of Alaska. As he sinks further into his chair, he becomes more sullen and quiet as the black outside invades the house and his soul. His wife, Ann, asks him if he's okay. He lies to her, "Yes." That's much easier than answering truthfully and getting into a big discussion about his heavy heart. Now is the time for Tom to enter himself and discover what really moves at his core, to learn what's really going on within him and to know and celebrate his real self. Here's how he does it:

He begins with the feeling and behavior signals. The feeling is gloom or depression. The behavior is loss of energy and silent sitting. These are Tom's top layers, the stuff that he sees and shows to the world. These cues are great starting points for his journey inward.

Basically Tom is going to ask himself two questions: *"Why?"* and *"Why is that important to me?"* He begins with the "Why?" question.

Question: Why are you feeling depressed?

Answer: Because it's Sunday night, and tomorrow I have to go back to work.

Question: And why is it depressing to you to go to work?

Answer: I like my time off. I enjoy leisure time.

Question: Why is it important for you to have and enjoy leisure time?

Answer: Because I don't like the rat race of work and all its demands.

Question: Why is it important for you not to get caught up in the rat race?

Answer: The rat race drains me. I lose energy. And I want more energy.

Question: Why is it important for you to have more energy?

Answer: Because if I have more energy, I can live a fuller, more satisfying life. That's what I want.

Question: Why is it important for you to live a more satisfying and fuller life?

Answer: Because I have such a short time on earth, I want my life to be the best I can make it.

Question: Why is it important to you to make your life the best you can make it?

Answer: I don't know. It's just part of me. It seems like I naturally want to have all that life can offer.

Tom experiences no further answers except to say "Just because . . . " or "It's part of my nature." When he can no longer answer the "Why-is-that-important-to-you" question, he has either gotten stuck in the process or he has reached his core energy. In this case he hit one of his core energies – namely the energy to *exist as best as he can.*

Tom began this process focused on his depression and gloom. As he journeyed through his beliefs, he touched a deep power within him – to be his best and fullest self. This orientation in him – this energy – needs to be celebrated by him, for it is very good. Thank goodness for the movement in him to be his best self. He may not be acting like he's being this "best self," but the energy is still there.

Tom's behaviors and feelings actually sabotage his energy toward fullness. Presently they are taking away his life. The energy deep within him is toward life. His behaviors and feelings pull him away from life. This lack of fit causes Tom stress. His outside does not match his inside.

Principle 11

For your sense of self choose to focus on your energies rather than on your behaviors or feelings.

Now Tom can focus either on his feelings of depression and gloom, or he can attend to the energy of his heart – the movement in him toward living the fullest life possible. He gives power to what he focuses on. Focusing on his loss of leisure time because work starts again tomorrow gives his depression greater power in his life.

Zeroing in on his energy to live life fully orients him into the present moment and allows him to give this Sunday evening his very best shot. The energy of his heart will literally energize him. Those energies are like built-in batteries. Whenever Tom feels run down and wiped out, he can turn to those deeply implanted batteries and re-charge the engine.

The deeper realization here, however, deals with self-esteem. Who is Tom? Is he his feelings of depression and gloom? Or is he the energy of being his best self? I vote for the latter. By identifying and focusing on the energy of his heart, Tom gradually learns he is those energies. He is not a depressed person. On the contrary, he is a man striving for the fullness of life but who is presently feeling sad because he doesn't believe he's satisfying that movement in him.

Don't give too much power to your behaviors and feelings. I know everyone else does. But please be counter-cultural here. Go against what is common. Use your energies as the basis for self-acceptance. Then even when you feel down or act unkindly, you won't beat yourself up. Beneath those actions and feelings lie wonderful energies that seek to surface in more positive and life-giving ways.

Principle 12

When using this structured approach to achieve higher self-acceptance overcome the four stumbling blocks to its success.

This process takes concentration and perseverance. You have to stay with it. If you know some of the obstacles along the way, you will be better prepared to conquer them.

1. Intense feelings

When you have very strong feelings, this process won't work well. Don't even try it at a time when emotion overwhelms you. Your father dies. Grief floods your heart. Don't engage this process immediately. Allow yourself to grieve; feel the depth of pain; remain in your tears. Gradually, as the power of your feeling subsides, you will be able to ask the "why" questions that can lead you to your core energies.

2. Stopping too soon

At times in this process you will get stuck in a particular layer. Because you're stuck, you may think you have reached your core. For instance, you continue to feel resentment toward a neighbor who cut down a tree on his property. The tree gave you great shade in the summer, and you continue to be upset because he never asked you how his decision would affect you. You keep on believing he should have asked your opinion before hacking down the tree. You can't get past that belief. So, of course, the resentment remains.

You ask yourself: "Why is it important to me that he consult with me before cutting down his tree?" No answer comes, except a strong belief that you'd like to cut *him* down inch by inch. You conclude that at your core lies *resentment*. You must be a resentful person. Whoa! Wait! That's too quick. You are not a resentful person. You have not gone deeply enough.

You must begin this process believing that every journey ends in a positive, life-expanding place. Your energies are good. They lead to life. If you get stuck short of that good place, then know only that you got stuck. You have not yet reached your center.

Take a little break. Accept that you simply got stuck. Maybe the resentment is still too strong. Perhaps you have a very strong belief about neighborly consultation. Try challenging your "right" to be consulted. See if you can't break down the power of your belief that your neighbor should have consulted you. And keep asking yourself what lies under the resentment. If there's resentment, there must be some value or energy deeper in you that struggles to surface.

3. No answers to the "why" questions

As you journey more deeply toward your core, answering the questions becomes more difficult. When you end up saying "I don't know," either you hit your core energies or you're stuck. There is an answer. You just don't know it yet. So don't give up too easily. When you hear yourself saying, "I don't know," stay with it. Keep searching for an answer.

You can usually get un-stuck by reversing the question, asking it in the negative. Let's say the question is: "Why is it important for you to feel a sense of accomplishment?" You don't know. An answer just doesn't come. Reverse the question. Ask it negatively. "What would happen if you failed to accomplish something you set out to do?" That usually shakes you loose. You will find an answer to that question and then be able to continue on the journey to your heart.

4. Focusing on others

Remember, the purpose of this process is to learn who *you* are and to *like* who you are. It's too easy to keep your attention on others. That's part of the problem for many people who don't like themselves. They never spend any time with themselves. They're always centered in others.

In working this process of self-acceptance and self-esteem, keep focused on you. During these few moments of the day you deserve to attend to yourself. To keep yourself directed toward you instead of others, make sure you always ask the questions like this: "Why is that important *for me?*" Example: You worry about your child. He's not very motivated regarding school. You can very easily get caught in why it's important *for him* to get better grades. But that's not the issue here. The question is: "Why is it important *for me* that my son be more motivated in school?" *You* are the object of this journey inward. If you focus on your son, you once again will be living on the outside of yourself. Remember, the journey is inward to your own heart.

Chapter Four

A Less Structured Approach to the Heart

You've had a chance now to work with the cognitive, step-by-step approach to reaching your heart. This method helps you get started in the search for your deepest energies. It also helps you identify those beliefs (layers) that facilitate or hinder the full development of your energies. Now I'd like to show you another approach to reaching your heart. It's less structured and more intuitive. It doesn't flow in the clear and precise manner of the structured approach. But you may find it more comfortable for you and more in sync with your own style of entering your self.

Principle 13

Enter whatever you experience.

In this approach nothing can interfere with the process, because nothing distracts. In other words, any information that comes to you, you incorporate as part of the process. You work with whatever thoughts, feelings and responses you have. All data are grist for the mill.

Consequently, do not fight against anything that comes to you. For example, you sit down to engage in this process, but all you can think of is the job project you are working on. It's due tomorrow, and you have so much more work to do yet. You don't really have the time to be sitting here trying to "journey to your heart." Your worry about the project stems from the comment of your boss about how he's depending on you regarding this project. You don't want to let him down. And you know if you do well, it will probably move your career along.

These thoughts and feelings keep racing through you. But you also want to get to your core energies. Do not see your thoughts and feelings about the work project as negative, bad or distracting. In fact, these are the very voices you want to work with. If you try to move away from these loud voices, they will simply re-occur. They are most important in your life right now. They are where you are at. So stay with them. Enter the voices, the thoughts and feelings, and see where they take you.

In this case, for instance, you enter your worry about the boss's approval. You allow yourself to really sense the worry. What does the worry feel like in you? Where in your body do you experience the worry? What thoughts do you have around the worry? Enter what you experience. Stay with it.

Principle 14

Believe that whatever you enter, you will pass through and exit to a deeper level.

Enter the worry! Why, you wonder, should you attempt to make yourself more worried? You want less, not more. You enter the worry because it has an important message for you about you. You don't want to focus on the worry in order to stay worried. But you do want to face your worry, to learn its message. Then you want to pass through it and out of it.

When you begin this process, believe and trust that whatever you enter you will pass through and exit. You need not be afraid that you will get stuck in your worry. By entering it and facing it, you will, paradoxically, more easily let it go. Why? Because your worry is a signal directing you to your heart. As you pass through your worry, you will be carried deeper within, closer to the energies of your heart.

So, you start this journey with two notions:

    1. You enter whatever comes to you;

    2. Trust that whatever you enter, you will pass through.

Principle 15

Start by asking yourself:
" (Name), who are you today?"

Remember, you *are* the energies of your heart. In journeying to your heart, then, you are discovering who you are. So begin by asking that question: "Who are you today?" It orients you to your journey's goal.

Well, who are you today? The worry immediately pops up. Your thoughts begin to race, centering on the work project. Worry, pressure, tension flood you. You enter your worry. You let yourself experience it. As you swim around in your anxiety, you realize you want to impress your boss. So you enter your desire to impress your boss. You sense that desire, that need to have your boss respond favorably to you. You imagine him doing so. But just as quickly you imagine him disapproving. That feels terrible.

If he disapproves, then you sense you will remain stuck in your present position. You're getting tired of your work and want a change. Now you focus on your desire for change. You enter it. You sense a little burst of energy when you think about changing work responsibilities. There has been no challenge in your present job for some time now. You feel bored. You like challenge and novelty. So you enter your interest and desire for new challenges.

That feels stimulating. It renews a sense of zest in your work life. You enter the zesty feeling. It tingles through your body. Thinking about and feeling the stimulation of change puts movement in your life. You realize you like change. You hate stagnation and mere repetition. You like new experiences. You like movement. You dwell in these feelings. They begin to fill you with an energy for living life to its fullest. You suddenly feel free. Before you felt trapped, dead-ended. Now you sense your life moving. You have steps to take, decisions to make. You no longer feel cornered. You let yourself dwell in the energy to move into life. You have the choice.

You like what you are now experiencing. You have, in fact, touched two energies. You have entered the energy to live life to its fullest and the energy to be free and in charge of your own life. Today, then, you are a free person who wants to live life to its fullest. That is *who* you are. As the day goes on, you may not always *act* that way, but nonetheless that is who you are.

Principle 16

Focus on your core energies in order to give them power.

Once you touch your core energies, you want them to grow in you. You give them power by attending to them, keeping your focus on them. You let yourself dwell in the experience of living life fully, accepting new challenges, being energized by them. You stay with the experience of freedom. You know you direct your own life. You realize you have choices and you want to make those choices.

One way of increasing that energy is to imagine the inside of you as a tiny dot of light. Your body is like a dark cavern. That little dot of light slowly begins to shine more brightly. It gradually fills that shadowy space with its brilliance. Soon your entire body is bathed in that light. Your core energies fill your body space. They flood your mind and take you over. You truly are your energies.

Principle 17

Now embrace and celebrate your energies.
For you are those energies.

At this point you want to affirm your core energies and yourself. You tell yourself: "Yes, this is who I am. I *am* a free person who wants to live a full, challenging and refreshing life. And it is good to be this person." Such an affirmation puts the exclamation point on this less structured process to your heart. You carry this awareness with you into your day. You are a free person. You want to *act* that way. You want to live and work making choices that move you to a fuller life experience, one in which you can enter new challenges and opportunities.

Since you have been focused on your core energies, you have de-powered your worry about that work project. The worry didn't simply vanish. In fact, my bringing the subject up again causes you to re-focus on the work project and rekindle the worry. But you did shift off the worry and actually gave power to your deeper energies. Focusing on your core energies regularly allows you to empower your deepest and best self and to de-power such experiences as worry, sadness and anger.

In using this process over the years personally and with many clients, I have noticed that people often cannot remember what their starting point was. They may have started with worry and gotten to living freely at their heart. When I asked them what feeling or thought they began this process with, they couldn't remember. From the beginning to the end of this process they had so moved their focus from the outer voice to the voice of their own energy that they actually could not recall the starting point.

Principle 18

Repetition makes this process easy.

I want to take you through another example of this process, because each journey is different. Each time you touch your energies, you get there by an uncharted path. This isn't a journey planned out precisely by your psychological travel agent. There is no map highlighting each road to take or what hotels to stop at along the way.

One Thursday morning I got up at 6:15. I showered, shaved, dressed, went down stairs, fed the cat, let the dog out, poured a glass of orange juice and retired to my den. The rest of the family was stirring upstairs. I had a few minutes to myself. I sat quietly in my chair and asked the question: "Dale, who are you today?" I let myself pay attention to whatever came to me.

Nothing seemed to come. But I knew that wasn't really possible, because I was at least aware that nothing was coming. So I started with that. I tried to enter "just sitting there with nothing coming in." It felt a little strange, somewhat uncomfortable. I wanted something to happen. I didn't have that much time and didn't want to waste it. I felt a little pressure in my forehead, wanting something to happen. But nothing was.

I just tried to stay with the experience. The longer I stayed with "nothing happening," the more frustrated I became. Ah, now there was a real feeling – frustration. I entered my frustration. I wanted something to happen. It wasn't. I got frustrated. I sensed myself banging my head against a wall. I let myself enter that experience – head banging. I imagined banging my head against a wall. The wall wasn't moving. My head began hurting. More frustration.

Next I became aware of wanting to be successful at this exercise because that evening I was giving a talk on this subject and wanted to use my morning's process as an example for the group. But what if I couldn't do it myself? The pressure was on to produce.

I felt empty. I didn't want that. I wanted to feel full of life and insight. I asked myself why I so wanted that sense of life and insight today? (This question came from the more cognitive, structured approach. Great. Use whatever you need to use.) I noticed a little flip in me at that time. I had been frustrated because my processing was going nowhere. I wanted to succeed, not so much for my own benefit today but because I wanted to demonstrate this process to my audience that evening.

I focused then on my desire to show this process to the group that evening. I became aware of a nurturing element within me. I wanted this group to understand this process and be able to use it. I stayed with that nurturing sense. I tried to keep focused on the nurturing movement rather than on "the group" I would be nurturing. (The focus in this exercise is always on the self, not on the other.) Yes, I realized I was a nurturer. That was who I was. Good. I wanted to build that sense. I saw the nurturing energy as that small dot of light slowly filling the cavern of my body-mind. I didn't let myself focus on nurturing that group but on just *being* a nurturing person, no matter who the object of the nurturing would be. I tried to sense the loving that moved within me. "Yes," I said, "I am a loving person and that is good."

Shortly after I completed this journey, my daughter, Amy, came downstairs. Since I was a loving person, that movement of love could and did get directed to her as the first object in my path. Amy got my love that moment. At work during the day, each of my clients became the object of my nurturing energy. At home after work, my wife and children became the object of that same loving nurturance. That night the audience for my talk became the object of my nurturing energy. Throughout the day, the objects of my nurturing energy changed. But my nurturing energy remained constant. I was a nurturing person.

There were, of course, times during the day when I didn't act out of my nurturance. The car driver who cut in front of me didn't receive my nurturing love. I was still a nurturing person, but I didn't act out of that nurturance. My behavior at that moment did not match the energy of my heart. Okay. I could work on my anger while driving. But, still, I was a nurturing, good person who got a little angry while driving.

The entire process I just described highlights a common difficulty in using this less structured approach. At times you will feel stuck. Either nothing comes to you, or you will feel mired in a deep, dark emotion. The more you stay with your stuck experience, the more frustrated you will become. Then go with the frustration. The frustration will move you along.

Principle 19

**Know the hints and cautions in using this
less structured approach.**

While this process can be highly energizing and extremely helpful in assisting you to reach your inner goodness, it holds some traps that can discourage you. Knowing them beforehand will help you get free if they ensnare you. So remember these hints as you enter this process:

Be patient.

Like any psychological process, this effort takes a fair amount of practice. Reading about it here may make it sound reasonable and helpful. Then you try it, and it doesn't seem to work as easily as it did when you read about it. (By the way, that's a problem with most psychology books. It looks easy on paper, but the practice is much more difficult.) So stay with it. You're trying to break through patterns that have been in place and practiced by you for years. It takes time.

If you feel stuck in the process, don't give up. Sometimes you will reach your core energies quickly and easily. Other times it will be a struggle. Remember, if you get stuck and stay with the stuck feeling, you will probably begin feeling frustration. So, pay attention to the frustration. Frustration signals a desire for something. Uncover that desire and enter it. By doing so you move into the desire for something (a fuller life, love, freedom). That moves you forward.

If the process takes longer at a particular time, don't worry about it. Your success is not measured by time spent. I worked once with a woman who spent three hours one morning in my office using this process to discover her inner energies. I also know that at other times the process can take one minute. So don't let time dictate your sense of success or failure.

Don't confuse "longing" with "energies."

Say, for example, that you miss your friend. She recently moved across the country. She seems so far away. You begin the focusing process. All you can think of is your friend and how much you miss her. You long for her. You conclude about yourself: "I am a person longing for Kate." No. You're not a longing-for-Kate person. You're a loving person who wants to direct your love right now toward Kate but can't because she is across the country. The longing focuses you on Kate.

Use the longing. Enter it. But go through it to the deeper energy. Your longing is a sign of your loving energy. Focus on your loving energy, and you will be filled with a caring power to direct toward those you meet here and now. If you focus on your longing for Kate, you will pine away and miss the fulfilling opportunities of love in the present.

Keep disconnecting the objects of your energies.

I've mentioned this a few times already. But it remains such a major stumbling block, I want to say it again. You give power to what you focus on. The purpose of this journey is to know, accept and love *yourself.* You can attend to others later.

Think of it as you would a lesson in English grammar. You are the *subject* of the sentence. Your core energy is the *predicate*. Other things, people, or your behavior are the *objects* of that sentence. Take the example above. You miss Kate. The sentence reads:

I	long for (love)	Kate, who moved away.
Subject	**Predicate**	**Object**

Keep your focus on the predicate, not the object. *You* are a loving person. As soon as you shift your attention to Kate, you move out of the journey to your heart. *You* are the deepest predicates of your heart. Stay with those predicates and celebrate them.

When stuck, look for the flip side.

When you get stuck in this process it's often because you have entered dark and heavy feelings. Fear, sadness, anger and worry can capture you and not let go. When that occurs and you can't shake free, then consider the flip side of those feelings or attitudes. The flip side is not the opposite characteristic but one that usually *goes along with* the present feeling.

For instance, you may feel stuck in your anger with someone. It keeps coming up every time you want to focus. You can't get through it to the next layer in you. Then ask yourself: "What characteristic usually goes along with anger that I can view more positively?" If you're angry, what other characteristic usually goes along with anger? I think the answer is "passion for living." Usually, if you get angry about things, there is also a drive in you for living fully.

Think of some other flip sides. If you are shy, you are also probably gentle. If you are sad from a significant loss, you are also loving. If you are stubborn, you are usually filled with conviction. If you worry about others, you are no doubt caring.

Look for these flips only if you get stuck. If you're moving along to ever deeper layers, let the process itself take you there. When you do get stuck and see the flip side, then focus on that flipped side. The journey should continue on more easily.

Principle 20

Know there are four energies of your heart.

Throughout this book, as you have thought about the energies of the heart, you've developed a sense of what your different energies are. I haven't wanted to identify them beforehand, because I hoped for your own discovery. Now, though, I want to label the energies so you know what you're looking for.

Over the years I have realized there are four energies of the heart. You are born with these energies. Your loved ones are, too. Even people you can't stand possess these energies. They might not always act out of them directly, but they do possess the very same energies you do. Here, then, are the four energies of your heart:

1. To exist

You are constantly moving toward existence. Certainly you seek physical life, but you also drive toward psychological and interpersonal existence as well. You want to be recognized and attended to. In fact, if you are not noticed, you begin to feel as though you literally do not exist.

2. To exist as best as you can

This energy moves you toward living a full life. You are a human being. There is a drive in you to be the best, fullest, most satisfied, contented, healthy human being possible. In part that is why you're reading this book. That behavior comes from the energy in you to be your very best self. The drive for peace, happiness, joy and well-being arises from this energy to be your best self.

3. To live freely

The beauty and awesomeness of your human life lies in your power to make choices. Having the freedom to say yes or no so fills the human spirit that war upon war has been fought to protect that power. You strive for the opportunity to make your own decisions, take control of your life and feel in charge of your own destiny. That energy in you is strong and wonderful.

4. To love

Based on the energy of freedom comes love. You realize that to love, you need to be free. You cannot force love. Remember when your parents used to tell you to apologize to your sister? You didn't feel sorry or loving. Parental force made the words come out but the words didn't express your sorrow or love.

Your loving energy has two sides. You move toward *caring* for others, giving yourself to them in loving ways. And you also seek a sense of *belonging*. You want to be a part of others' lives. You want a feeling of being included, being cared for. This energy moves most powerfully in you. Over your lifetime you will experience this energy more consistently and persistently than the other energies. However, the others serve as the base for this powerful drive.

So those are the four energies. You might wonder if there couldn't be more than those four. All I can say is that over the years of my life experience and psychotherapy practice these four continue to surface as the families of energies. I say "families" because many nuances of these energies appear. For instance, the loving energy may take on the nuance of nurturing, challenging, encouraging, sympathizing, pursuing, gathering, protecting. All the energies will continually surprise you as you enter them, get to know them and celebrate them.

Allow yourself to stand in awe of these wonderful energies that make you who you are. If you keep your eyes and heart open as you journey to your heart, you will be surprised and amazed at what you find. You will like it, too.

Principle 21

Enjoy the fact that you have the same energies as everyone else.

"What's the big deal having these energies if everyone else has the very same ones?" Gene complained. "That doesn't make me any different than anyone else." In one sense Gene was right. Insofar as all people possess the same energies, they are the same as Gene. So what? Then everyone is fundamentally a good person with strong and valuable energies churning within.

What makes you different from Gene and everyone else is those layers. Your beliefs and attitudes, learned over the years, mix with your energies, and so you express yourself in very different ways from the ways other people do. Being different does not make you good or worthwhile. Being different only makes you different. That's nice. Thank goodness everyone is different. But what is basically good about you and the rest of us is precisely that we have the same core energies. These energies are good, so we are all good. We all act very differently, though, because of the layers that have conditioned those energies.

Focus on your energies to determine your goodness. Attend to your layers, behaviors and feelings to recognize the differences between you and others. Celebrate the inner goodness as well as the differences.

Principle 22

Once you reach your energies, stay with them.
Do not return to your behaviors too quickly.

Being a practical person, you will have a tendency to touch your core energies and quickly want to bounce back up to your behaviors, feelings and the outside world. Staying at the core doesn't always feel like you're getting anywhere. Resist the temptation to surface too quickly. By focusing on your energies, you give them power. They will rise up through the layers as they gather strength.

This entire journey to the heart moves in a U-shaped manner. The bottom of the U is your dwelling place. You don't want to come up from that U too quickly. You go down one side of the U, through the many layers of your life, in the effort to touch your core energies. After you live there for a period of time, you need to surface again, coming up the other side of the U.

Unfortunately, many people turn this U-shaped journey into a V-shaped process. They merely touch their core energies and spring right back to the top again, living in that noisy, other-focused world.

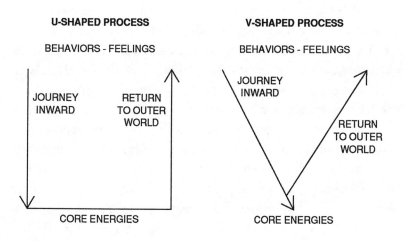

U-SHAPED PROCESS

BEHAVIORS - FEELINGS

JOURNEY
INWARD   RETURN
                  TO OUTER
                  WORLD

CORE ENERGIES

V-SHAPED PROCESS

BEHAVIORS - FEELINGS

JOURNEY
INWARD
                  RETURN
                  TO OUTER
                  WORLD

CORE ENERGIES

Concentrate on remaining quiet within yourself, focused on who you are and on your energies. Resist the urge in you to jump out of your heart into the world of behaviors and feelings. Interfere with the natural question: What do I do with this energy now that I know it's there? The answer will come in due time. Your job is simply to stay with the energy.

Principle 23

When you know yourself at the heart, then trust that you will know how to act.

The volcano erupts when enough energy builds up in the bowels of the mountain. No one needs to call the molten force of fire to rise. It ascends when the energy can no longer be contained by the walls of the mountain. Out it comes with force.

Acting out of your core energies stands as the final step in the journey inward. You journey inward in order to appreciate who you are and to act and feel in harmony with your heart's energy. The action that springs directly from your heart spells integrity. When you behave in harmony with your heart's energy, then you possess integrity. Your outside matches your inside.

To make that happen, you can use two methods. The first is the *explosion* approach. Like the volcano, the more power you give to your inner energies, the more likely those energies will explode through any belief layers that restrict and inhibit their course. You know the experience.

You're attending an important meeting on an important subject with important people. Some folks begin presenting a view that takes off. The meeting is moving in a direction you don't like. You feel strongly about your position, which isn't being heard. But you're very shy, especially around "important" people. You struggle with yourself. You ought to say something. You can't get yourself to do so. Finally, in a burst of energy – you don't know its source – you jump in and speak your mind with conviction and even passion.

Your inner energy broke through some shy layers in you. It exploded into behavior that matched your heart. Whether your point of view was well received or not, you walked away from that meeting with a sense of integrity. Your behavior matched your heart. That's the explosion process. The more you focus on your energies, the more power you give them. And the more likely those energies will emerge in behaviors that clearly reflect those energies.

The second approach in allowing your energies to surface has to do with the belief layers. To get through a wall, you can either generate enough force to charge right through it, or you can dismantle that wall brick by brick. In the explosion process you charge right through the wall. In the second approach you take the wall away so you can pass through more easily.

First you must recognize what the belief layers are. Those that inhibit the flow of energy have to be cut away. By doing so, you free your heart's energy. That energy can then ascend in you, easily and directly. You can eliminate those restrictive layers by challenging their accuracy, by fighting to disbelieve them and by learning to think new, more positive beliefs. (Ways of doing this are found in the **Life Skills Series** book, *Thinking Reasonably.*)

Chapter Five

Developing this Skill with Others

Because of the detours and little traps along the path to your heart, working with another on this skill will help you considerably. As you already have experienced in working with this book, it's easy to get stuck along the way. Walking the path with another will help you amplify the whispers of your heart. Here are some suggestions for working with another person or a group:

Step One

Working in two's, one person facilitates the other's journey inward. Using the cognitive approach, the facilitator asks the "Why" questions. Remember the first question is: "Why do you feel that way, or why did you behave that way?" Use the cone diagram, have the journeyer respond out loud and write down his or her answers. Once the why is known, the facilitator then asks the "Why is that important *to you?* " questions. Keep doing this until the other hits a core energy. Then invite that person to remain at the core, affirm him or herself and celebrate being a full, free and loving person.

Or, using the intuitive, less structured approach, facilitate the other by encouraging that person to simple "Enter whatever you are experiencing" and "Stay with your experience." The other tells you only enough for you to be able to track with him or her. Say to the person: "Tell me only a little, just enough so that I have some sense of where you are." As you go along you may find you're having trouble following the person's journey. Then ask: "Please tell me what's going on for you right now."

When you do the less structured process with each other, encourage the one doing the journey to close his or her eyes. With the cognitive approach that person needs to write, so the eyes should stay open.

Step Two

After the process has been completed, debrief it with each other. Talk about what happened. At the end of the debriefing ask what was helpful and not helpful in your facilitating. This is a learning process for the facilitator, too. After you do this with the same person for a while, you will both get better at tracking with each other.

Step Three

Encourage each other to stay close to the heart and not bounce up to behaviors and feelings too quickly.

Step Four

Report to each other on your journey experiences during the week. Share your successes and your difficulties in reaching your core. Talk about ways to get through the stuck spots.

Step Five

Also review how much you lived with integrity during the week. Celebrate those many integral actions and learn from those times when you failed to live faithfully to your heart. You will notice how frequently your behavior is, in fact, in harmony with your heart. Most of your daily life is lived with integrity. Learn to celebrate that fact. Sharing it with others allows the celebration of your life to continue.

Step Six

Encourage one another to live for integrity and not for joy, to be faithful to the whisper of the heart and not the noise of the world. Celebrate each other's existence as good and magnify the voice of each other's heart by your own free and loving behavior.

Conclusion

We have walked with one another for a time. Our journey has taken you inward to the awesome awareness of powers that make you good and wonderful. I believe this about me and I believe this about you – we are good people. Continue the journey. Don't give up when the road curves and the night comes. The whisper within and the tiny dot of light are always there to guide you.

Review of Principles for Accepting Yourself

1. Self-acceptance and self-esteem are found *within* yourself, not outside of yourself.
2. All creation is made up of outer and inner voices. Learn to listen most attentively to your own inner voice.
3. Your inner voice can be framed also as the voice of God or of your Higher Power.
4. Your inner voice speaks of positive energies.
5. Your outer voices are made up of all the messages you have received throughout your life and incorporated within.
6. You need to know the relationship between the outer voices and the energies of the heart.
7. Feelings are not part of your core energy. They exist at the outer edge of your being.
8. Self-acceptance and self-esteem are based on your ability to focus on your core energies rather than on your behaviors or feelings.

9. To enter your heart, begin with your behaviors and feelings.

10. There are two ways to reach the heart. First, you can proceed, layer by layer, in a cognitive, structured way. Second, you can move in a less structured, more intuitive way.

11. For your sense of self choose to focus on your energies rather than on your behaviors or feelings.

12. When using this structured approach to achieve higher self-acceptance overcome the four stumbling blocks to its success.

13. Enter whatever you experience.

14. Believe that whatever you enter, you will pass through and exit to a deeper level.

15. Start by asking yourself: "(Name), who are you today?"

16. Focus on your core energies in order to give them power.

17. Now embrace and celebrate your energies. For you are those energies.

18. Repetition makes this process easy.

19. Know the hints and cautions in using this less structured approach.

20. Know there are four energies of your heart.

21. Enjoy the fact that you have the same energies as everyone else.

22. Once you reach your energies, stay with them. Do not return to your behaviors too quickly.

23. When you know yourself at the heart, then trust that you will know how to act.